PERU

HERBERT MORRIS

MIDDLEBURY COLLEGE LIBRARY

HARPER & ROW, PUBLISHERS, New York
Cambridge, Philadelphia, San Francisco, London
1817   Mexico City, São Paulo, Sydney

PS
3563
.087434
P4
1983

"The Road" first appeared in *The Kenyon Review.*
"The Treason of the Clerks Takes Many Forms" and "Fifty-ninth Street" first appeared in *The Hudson Review.*
"My Double in a Drama Filmed in France," "Being a Soldier," "At the Hotel Where the Long Dark Begins," and "Scriabin" first appeared in *American Review.*
"Newport, 1930," and "These Are Lives" first appeared in *The Paris Review.*
"Thinking of Darwin" first appeared in *The Virginia Quarterly Review.*
"The French Night" first appeared in *The New Yorker.*
"Palm Beach, 1928" first appeared in *Shenandoah: The Washington and Lee University Review.*
"When the Silence Becomes Too Much to Bear" and "History of China" first appeared in *Antaeus.*
"How to Improve Your Personality," "Havana," "Waiting for Marguerite," "River Road," and "After the Reading" first appeared in *New England Review.*

PERU. Copyright © 1983 by Herbert Morris. All rights reserved. Printed in the United States of America. No part of this book may be used or reproduced in any manner whatsoever without written permission except in the case of brief quotations embodied in critical articles and reviews. For information address Harper & Row, Publishers, Inc., 10 East 53rd Street, New York, N.Y. 10022. Published simultaneously in Canada by Fitzhenry & Whiteside Limited, Toronto.

FIRST EDITION

Designer: Sidney Feinberg

Library of Congress Cataloging in Publication Data

Morris, Herbert, date
  Peru.
  Poems.
  I. Title.
PS3563.087434P4 1983   811'.54   82-48128
ISBN 0-06-015116-1   83 84 85 86 87 10 9 8 7 6 5 4 3 2 1
ISBN 0-06-091020-8 (pbk.)   83 84 85 86 87 10 9 8 7 6 5 4 3 2 1

Contents

For my mother
and
my father
and
my brother

The Road

I like the story of the circus waif
bought by the man-of-weights to be his mistress,
Profit the demon dragging her to market
and Lust the soul who paid in lire for her.

I like the peculiarities of her faith,
the startling quality of that innocence,
kissing the hand that dealt her cruelty
believing, poor and dumb, that this was love.

I relish a destitution stripped to sing
pure in a voice all passion and denial:
such are the driven burning by their breath
more than mere air allows and cold permits.

I savor my own involvement and concern
lest all the transformations seem unreal,
lest love be painted water-sweet and classic
rather than salt and anguish to the end.

I like her squatting in the village road
combing the dust for something of her own,
coming away belonging and committed,
roots to be cherished, stones she could befriend.

And what I like the subtlest and profoundest
is that the circus traveled grief to grief
educating the waif into a woman
loving and beautiful and fiercely proud.

I think of the sense of fury in that road,
stooping to scratch the earth out for a life
somewhere awaiting finding in one's name.
I like that, and I like the word Expense.

I think of the years together which they had,
the strong-man working her into the act,
that hint, despite himself, of some devotion.
I like that, and I like the ring of Cost.

Not in a root, or stone, but in a man
she found a thing to hold her tenderness.
I like her dedication after that,
her saying, if she spoke, I live by this.

And what I like pervasive and forever
is that my eyes have wept the tale before,
wanting the telling not so much as story
but for the way the waif befits my life.

The Treason of the Clerks Takes Many Forms

All day, perched on high stools, they tallied numbers
that bore no small resemblance to their lives.
All day, and year to year, they peered, they summed,
and something in the clock tooled their reduction.

All day they seemed exemplars of compliance.
All day pale figures issued from their pens.
The attics creaked, the water-spouts ran rusty,
and rain would seep like acid in the street.

All day the overseer lashed their backs
with scowls like cuts and scrutinies like salt.
But there were freezes faces might resort to,
havens the bones could posit, grins like refuge.

All day some Middle Europe of the mind
possessed them, leaked into the ink-pots, doubled
what darkness doomed the sashes, the disdain
of the dim overseer in his frockcoat.

All day the cold besieged the Gothic angles
and something in the blood, too bleak too thin,
could, at best, muster nothing in rebuttal.
Words choked within the throat, the mouth poured ashes.

But what the overseer could not know,
the gutter-spouts, the light that ate the stones,
was that the darkness, intimate and fleet,
released them to themselves, yielded the other.

In the night, after they replaced each ledger
on the high shelf, scrubbed at their fingers, after
partaking, near the grate, of musty suppers,
shriveled fruit picked at by the blind street-vendor,

their dank and rancid woolens were transformed
to something greenly flowing, nearly silken.
Their hands, no longer cramped, sullied with ink-dye,
opened like flowers, breathed and beat like wings.

And the night was given to deeper things,
to darker things, to forces that, like music,
structured the universe in affirmations
of the intensest kind until the morning.

Where they would walk or lie, and where their bodies
knew as if for the first time, night to night,
what the body was made for, that the mouth
was human and a mouth, articulation

broke out like light in the most alien corners,
after that could not hope to be contained.
Their faces seemed, at last, redeemed as faces,
their lives gained all the meanings of a life.

By daybreak every dampness infiltrated,
great bone-chill drew its stores and settled in.
All odor of the field, all hint of wildness,
now was turned back, plowed under, burned, annulled.

They groped through certain foul, corrosive lanes,
gripping the rain's raw anguish in their teeth.
They found the door, climbed stairs, lit a poor fire.
Closer they drew their coats, to no avail.

Over their desks they bent their heads and summed.
The water in their hair defaced the sheets.

The overseer lashed, resumed the war.
The gutter-spouts streamed poisons, as before.

All day they seemed the model attic scribblers.
All day they tasted ash and reeked of dread.
The body knows deceptions long and lucid.
The night is deeper than the dead are dead.

My Double in a Drama Filmed in France

I knew you afternoons in railway stations
whose single-track trunk lines run dusty, late,
between one desolation and another,
you in the most ill-fitting uniform
issued by a once-proud Italian army,

sipping a coffee at an outdoor table
with a young girl who wished to be your sister
in a cold, gutted room above the station
for the brief hour before your train's arrival,
or a woman who thought she was your mother.

I knew you by the placement of those hands
before you on the table, hands that sifted
light in them like white bowls in northern windows,
a strange, mild sun lapping the province that day,
blinding the eyes of the piazza's statue,

warming us who were never wholly warm,
teaching us light who had not been taught light.
To the south, rumors of profound defeat
continued circulating through the morning
with the arrival of the dispossessed

by coach and van, their packs slung on their backs,
carpets and mattresses lashed to gaunt horses.
In the confusion, little would seem lost
but the long waiting which became our lives.
I knew you where the dust began to dance,

the roar of cannons, din of mortarfire
suddenly drawing closer in its focus,
the troops of forces called the enemy,
according to reports, reaching the outskirts
by daybreak of that morning we awake

to understand, I think for the first time,
who we are, where the battle has been fought,
in some dim breach that everything depended
not on the reinforcements' late arrival
but somewhere on one's way of saying yes.

That evening, in a room above the station,
absence would sing as sweetly as a presence
on the cold, rusting springs to which it clung,
the dark-haired girl go out to seek a brother,
the older woman sleep with other sons.

The day the peace was signed, when you came home
through the baroque of that shell-battered station
where much of what we dreamt had taken place,
I knew you where the cuff exposed the wrist
and where the collar spoke too much of neck,

where what seemed you and what seemed uniform
walked each distinctly the Italian dusk,
the vast smoke of the last provincial light
filtering through the nakedness between.
I knew you knew the route that rent the night.

Newport, 1930

Stepping deftly to the jetty,
members of the boating party,
women in pearls, long skirts, cloche hats,
men in blazers, white yachting flannels,
slickers dangling from an arm,

walk the ramp to the misty shore.
The sand is grey, the water greyer,
the light a queasy off-grey color
depriving everything of shadow.
The time must be late afternoon,

the day unlike the day in summer,
given the variables, it must be.
Crews from the offshore yawls and sloops,
maneuvering small white-hulled tenders
ferrying members of the party,

are dressed as that year's crews are dressed,
are seen to do what ships' crews do.
Though their hands are unseen by us
(the distance, yes, but greyness, too)
we are given to understand

(I cannot yet fully explain it)
nowhere will they prove less than equal
to whatever is asked of them:
hold to the wheel, haul port, trim starboard,
cast these members ashore, man stations.

A small flag flutters from the stern of
each of the auxiliary tenders.
Could we count the stars splattered on them
we could, within specific limits,
narrow the context, taste the year.

Of the life of those party members
put ashore on the coast of twilight,
walking in twos into that evening
where the evening is spread before them
like the fall of a woman's hair,

what can I say but that this woman,
after the dusk has fallen, late,
somewhere not far from sea-routes, sailor,
where the choices pertain to voyage,
lets down her hair as dark as water;

that the man who accompanies her,
armed with a slicker against sheer downpour,
soon, with the night and tide propitious,
sails out on what, not far from here,
the woman has let down like water;

that the hands of the crew, no matter
how astonishing that insight
into the reach of their commitment,
in the long darkness founder, crumble,
finger by finger leak with dust.

From the balustrade we view them
moving together into contexts
of which we have nothing but outlines:
fleets in the bay riding at anchor,
tenders plying their final runs,

the first stars tangled in the rigging,
belowdeck crews taking their suppers;
that entering on darkness, darkness,
the absence, voyager, of shadows;
that letting down, somewhere, of hair.

Being a Soldier

Stan Smith at Forest Hills

It must be to be squinting in the sun,
must be at the conclusion of the set
to leap across the net wearing success
as though it were familiar and accustomed,

the face it seems the face one always wore,
the perspiration knifing down the back,
the regulation shirt stained, body-clinging.
It must be to be young, it must be winning.

It must be lying evenings in the barracks
being indistinguishable from the others,
in underwear with one's name stenciled on it
listening to the guitar six cots down,

to be stationed near Indianapolis
or somewhere equally removed from water
where twilight takes a long time in the cornfields
and the girls order milkshakes at the drive-ins.

In the sun it must be to come to power,
to move as though such endless barracks waiting,
nights sweet with June, July, seem not excessive
if in time it means it may come to this:

last-minute rallies flawless for their timing,
leaning into returns with crucial skill,
impeccable the intricate half-volleys,
slowing the serves to thwart a rival's forehand.

It must be to lie back in Pasadena
(that California of the life or mind)
examining the trophies on a shelf
where the last half-light kindles little fires

in the depth of the bowls of golden cups
or rages through the cool rows of medallions
where silver waits to be touched by that life.
It must be to be twenty-four and blond.

Sipping champagne sent by the racket maker,
"The Army has been good to me," one mutters,
one hears oneself explaining to reporters,
forgetting the anonymous guitars,

not mentioning the nights of barracks waiting,
the suns such long time going down, the golden
girls drinking butterscotch milkshakes at the drive-ins,
those Indianas severed from the sea.

It must be to go home and, like the rest,
to lie alone at evening, to be dreaming
hammering cross-court, playing into darkness
no evening falls sufficient to bring down,

a wind raking the ankles, private's sweat
whose salt-lash eats the lips, dreaming two wrists
dazzling enough to light one through that life
where night, like justice, inundates the courts.

Thinking of Darwin

Were it not for that photograph,
disaster in its final stages,
matchbox houses coming down,
rubble of streets, uprooted trees,
lives we somehow could not envision,
removed from us and not our own,
on distant coasts the fall of night,

we might never have thought of Darwin,
remembered what we had forgotten,
nothing but desert at our backs,
somewhere the light gone grey, gone green,
the very texture of the air
evoking strangeness in us, distance,
deepwater harbor on the rim
of an island whose aspirations,
despite itself, assume proportions
hemispheric, continental,
set adrift in uncharted waters
where a wind from the Timor Sea
smacks of Celebes, of Java,
celebrates archipelagoes
for which no names have been devised,

where rain runs green, and rocks dream gold,
where every morning, on our tongues,
we taste the raging of the dust
gathering at abandoned stations

and know, or come to know, the life,
the littoral on which we wait,
though not yet clearly its true name,
not precisely its purpose with us;

where, naked, night to night, inventing
names for our nakedness, we lie
suspended under the Equator
between the wastes of self and weather,
trying to learn ourselves, our names,
what to make of this emptiness,
this sense of absence which afflicts us,
forgetting what we must remember,

the great Australian coast spun out
beyond our scrutiny in shales,
corals, limestones, salt scrub, sand,
discovery at every turn
and, this far south, no turning back,
latitudes of impossible
dimensions bleaching the horizon,
mapping what will not quite stay mapped,
nothing but desert at our backs,
nothing but darkness to advance on,
night on the routes that enter strangeness
more dangerously, in the evening,
than we can bring ourselves to say,
darkness and an interior
for which, of course, there is no name
except, unmapped, unknown, ourselves.

Fifty-ninth Street

Henry James was enjoying
that success we reject in calling modest,
horse-drawn carriages clattered through the streets,
and snow, when there was snow,
muffled the very rhythm of the city.

The Plaza, or a castle like it,
loomed as the centerpiece in dreams
which Fifty-ninth Street dreamt that year,
wild brush and scrub still to be cleared,
those evenings it was given to
abandoning itself to dreams
of French châteaux, gilt ballrooms, chandeliers,
the great stones lapped by light, a fierce, pure light,
where the moon rose like strangeness in the park,
and the foundations going down to bedrock.

My father, on a train from Cincinnati,
slept with his palm pressed to his cheek,
eleven years crammed in a small valise
swaying on the luggage rack above him,
boy in a thin wool suit with brown tweed knickers,
dreaming those dreams of clearing the uncleared,
dreaming, from the beginning, Fifty-ninth Street,
moonlight, the snow, tomorrow in those streets
each tracking north, pronouncing the same word:
                    uptown.

Beyond the strangeness of the park,
fields of the-still-to-be-explored,

past the long, crooked arrow, Broadway,
on which the island lay impaled;
where the river, named for a Dutchman
who probed the bay and, dreaming north,
risked openings to self, to north,
glittered even on moonless nights,
approaches to the bridge had not yet
bitten deep into cliffs lining the river,
nor had the red lighthouse been built
at the point where the span, above, would soar—

all of it salt marsh, forest, squatters' shacks,
men on both shorelines fishing through the ice.

Precisely what the river dreamt
as the fishermen drilled their holes,
deftly let down improvised lines;
as the snow settled in the streets,
carriages plodding north on missions,
from this distance, undetermined;

what the water may have been dreaming
as the moon rose from that dense tangle
of self and strangeness called the park;
as the express from Cincinnati
kept to its schedule through the night,
one has no way, of course, of knowing.

My father, on the night coach from Ohio,
stirred in the dark and looked to his valise.

Somewhere, evenings, not far from Fifty-ninth Street,
slowly setting those traps in which the novel
later would find itself for all time snared,
James was advancing on that complication
of discipline and passion we call art,
advancing on the strangeness of the park
which, in the dark, is one's own strangeness, too,

that wilderness of motives, anguish, vision,
false starts, wrong turns, that dream of the uncleared,
those boundaries of the unnamed, unexplored,
my father, as a boy, called Fifth-ninth Street,
probes of the coast, openings to the north,
estuary farther than Albany
where the river dreams what a river dreams
before the bridge throws its shadow across it.

These Are Lives

One could as well have chosen
that life of supermarket carts
junked in the backyard,
where you stand and wait
with your mechanic's hands
and a bare chest
in summer, light
behind you jammed into the picture,
its code undecipherable
even by the camera,
so steep and dense its
dreaming smeared on the warped
boards of the toolshed, makeshift
cinder path, and what once must have been
grass of a lawn now given way
to automobile parts and that complication
of wreckage, brutal and casual
at once, whose talent it is to attach
itself to us in California
or to those lives in other places
we accede to.

Where evening finds us
I cannot name yet; these are lives
best seen, or dreamt, beneath that sun
of backyard chaos
and indeterminate nourishing power,
that sun of rusting crankshafts,
of beached headlights, where you wait

for what shall not be named yet in this poem,
where evening finds us,
should it find us,
on a second-hand mattress whose bent springs
jangle when the wind lies right,
those mechanic's hands
to small avail
against the infinite
machine turning
the stars on over California,
the dark no doubt insisting moonlight
color chaos silver soon in backlots
where supermarket carts
and auto bodies
await, if we are gifted,
restoration at our hands
(and we are gifted),
we who, beneath that daylight etched
like anniversaries on the calendar
nailed to the toolshed wall,
wait for what has not disclosed its name,
neither in California
nor in this life of bleached,
unlikely places.

The French Night

Seeing them merely moving from the car
to the fine ambiguity of woods,
where you know road somewhere stops being road
and begins, in the half-light, being night,
you know, of course, what you have always known:

never will there be darkness quite like this.
Even before the night has wholly fallen,
what you sense, not yet saying how you sense it,
is the burden of dusk finding their shoulders,
the scent of French verbs heavy on the air,

the particular texture of the evening
in that province whose name you think you know
but wish neither to tell yet nor be told,
the wilderness beginning to unravel,
darkness, but more than darkness, coming down.

But the car, moments later, where the roadsides
take a momentous turn to something else,
that something else which shall not yet be named,
seems no longer the means by which they came,
vague in a foreground overwhelmed with vagueness;

the woods, if one is certain they are woods,
doubling in fever, chill, have passed from woods
into a wisdom bordering on strangeness,
their dark the darkness of the still unentered
whose name, of course, remains to be disclosed;

and the road, which in French is not a road
but the articulation of becoming,
leading out of before and into after,
places them neither there nor there but here,
the sum of what you know and need to know.

Who they are, where they travel, why the dark
assumes dimensions, fluent on their shoulders,
darkness has never quite assumed before,
has to do with the French, with the French night,
with what one knows, what one has always known:

never will there be darkness quite like this,
the car, stricken with shadow, not a car,
the woods, profoundly altered, more than woods,
the road, at some extreme, transcending road,
that darkness more than darkness coming down.

Not really certain where they may be going,
not even certain they wish to be certain,
they move, step from the car, evening to evening
ask of evening only that it come down,
only that possibility assail them

in that far reach of field in French called lives,
ready to bear the strangeness of their breathing,
to approach the name of the ground they stand on,
waves of the French night breaking, wave on wave,
and context, context, all night coming down.

Palm Beach, 1928

It will be in the steps the meaning lies
leading away from where they may be going
or into what they are about to come from
One is uncertain
                    which is as it should be

All that one knows is the not visible
photographer with his machine requesting
that they both hold those smiles a moment longer
My uncle's feet grip firmly to the terrace
flagstones saying for all time Florida
His shoes are brown and white
                            gleam at the wingtips
with refractions of a tropical sun
shoes you know a boy buffed that very morning
My aunt's feet hold less firmly to their ground
more tentatively
                in pale lemon pumps
the right knee deftly bent (her contribution
rather than the photographer's one guesses)
softening the long sweep from hip to ankle

What one reads in their faces seems obscure
My uncle hardly squints beneath that sun
(all at once one wants to say conflagration
to ask how he can keep from being blinded)
has full cheeks
            curly hair
                 dark brows
                      good teeth

Aunt Paula's cloche protects her from the glare
its thin half-moon of shade veiling those eyes
that see whatever there will be to see
Accessories include a string of pearls
a hat and bag to match pale lemon pumps
a bow pinned to her chest of the same print
flowers and fruit
                    from which the dress is cut

I think she knows they stand in Florida
(something about her posture hints of that
that she is happy
                    that if there were words
they would be simply this
                              we are together)
I think she has agreed to call it that
never doubting Florida suits it best
never needing to ask what one might call it
if some morning
                    freed of all preconceptions
great weights suddenly lifted from the eyes
one approached it and dared not call it that
risked something darker
                    whispered its true name

After the photographer has released them
they will choose to go sailing
                              play golf
                                        swim
choice after choice make choices
                                    every morning
enter on what will darken to an evening
advance on what will gather to a life
She will be happy
                    they will be together
here where the steps both give out and take in

From the density of their seamless shadows

pressing one to another as in life
one knows morning breaks hot and faultless here
there is not a cloud in the sky
                              nothing
will intervene between them and the sun
a sun hammering fiercely on their shoulders
as the morning deliciously surrenders
to the unknown
                    to what is possible
finding them if it finds them on the route
to afternoon
                  to evening
                              where the dark
sings one song
                  embarkations
                              embarkations
where the night takes it all and takes it deep

Florida reaches out in all directions
what one agrees now to call Florida
but what one senses transcends name or place
Somewhere one knows a blue sea must be sounding
Somewhere a glimpse of virgin beach could blind us
The lawns are manicured
                              the gardens watered
At dusk each bush is trimmed
                                        each shrub is clipped
At dawn before the guests make their appearance
on the verandah sipping morning coffee
the grounds are swept
                        the borders kept from slipping
into their natural state of disarray

The backdrop of it all is this hotel
which they either arrive at or depart from
(the choice seems ours as much as it seems theirs)
where they will come to understand the evening
the nature of what may be possible

as it shall be given to understand
this arrangement of pink Italian sandstone
hauled by Addison Mizener from Carrara
and Spanish arches under which they winter
whose balustrade we just barely perceive
(no wind rustles the date palm on the terrace
the grounds are swept

                     the borders kept from chaos)
but whose steps

               dazzling white marble steps
leaving and entering at the same time
leading

        misleading

               holding fast

                     now yielding
cut to last at least several thousand years
but changing in the sun moment to moment
loom as the cornerstone of all we know
and all (the greater part) we do not know

cause us five decades later to suspend
any determination of direction
Uncle Ed and Aunt Paula may have taken
splendid figures on a bleached littoral
into the hot and faultless halls of weather
into the lanes of dust we call their lives
admit we know too little to envision
afternoon now no longer afternoon
garden no longer garden

                   sea not sea
that Florida we have agreed to call it
though at dusk we mean infinitely more
what they did when the dark fell

                    who they were

When the Silence Becomes Too Much to Bear

In the dark of morning it will read 4:00
on the clock all night ticking in your head,
after the dream in which, indelibly,
M has been put to shame by the conductor
on the night train barreling coast-to-coast
at a speed both magnificent and eerie,
seemingly with no stations in-between.

What you will slowly come to understand
is that, on an assembly-line in mill towns
perched ominously on those fierce, tight hills
where nothing grows, where nothing hopes to grow,
that place both more than place and less than place
where the hands give themselves to vast, exotic
systems of valve-shafts, pistons, bearings, gears,

someone has failed to hammer destination
into the bolts and nuts of this compartment:
the night train runs all night, but not on dreams.
More slowly still you come to understand
it is too soon to call it understanding:
what, for example, are to be the boundaries
of that quest, that immaculate pursuit,

in which pure knowledge of the very nature
of M's infraction, of infraction itself,
intricate, shining, changeless, dense with light,
at evening, where the continent's last stations

go up in smoke, shall be apparent to us,
revealed not because it is made more simple
but that a way to see is made more pure.

Is the conductor angered by M's dying,
chagrined that silence make such falling sound?
Are the eyes looking in instead of out,
bones, through the skin, becoming too transparent?
Or, in that half-sleep, is the passenger
repeating, note by note, some private music
of trunk-lines, way-stops, night-routes, embarkations,

Madrid, Shiraz, Mégève, Baku, Palermo,
those who have lived another life repeat,
as though not quite yet able to be torn
from music, that astonishment of music
at the abandoned junctions down the line
equal, somewhere, to this: Montevideo.
The night train runs all night, but not on dreams.

In the wastes of acute accelerations,
beat of the heart, weight of the dark, strange engines,
it will read after 4:00 when the conductor,
needing to separate us from our music,
root out all memory of Buenos Aires,
telegraphs ahead to the stationmaster
who, he believes, stands watch miles down the track.

What the message insinuates eludes us,
though it will have to do with M, with travel
in the country of our relinquishing:
Troublesome Passenger Persists in Dying
Quietly on the Night Train between Stations.
What Do I Do, What Does Anyone Do?
Miles down the track, no one will make response.

In the long dark, needing to know what danger
imperils the conductor, M, myself,

---

on the express that shuttles coast-to-coast
without cessation, without intervention
(although I know, on the night train I know);
famished for light, that opulence of stations
in the dream streaming all night from M's mouth,

cities, names for a continent of cities,
in my seat I turn slowly, see M's face
as beautiful as it has ever been,
at the lips the dim start of a fine mist
blurring distinctions between self and smoke,
overtaking the burden of that music
beginning, all night, all night, Valparaiso.

History of China

Which do you choose? China was asked that year,
when they gave names to who we are, and where,
when, for all time, our fates were locked in that,
the sin of not enough or that of excess.

I

In the northernmost provinces, one season,
they undertook the building of a wall
in a field where a full moon grazed the trees
like a riderless horse with a white mane.

It was a summer evening, warm and clear,
but by the time the wall had entered mountains,
foothills folded like crumpled paper flowers
one over the other, province to province,
by the time each brick was secured in place,
mountain giving to wall and wall to mountain,
it was no longer evening, it was night.

In China darkness goes by those two names,
depending on the strangeness of the province
and on one's life the moment strangeness finds him.

II

Sticks were whittled of pine bark, teak, bamboo.
They walked the woods for miles, seeking out cypress
young enough to be worked beneath their blades,
mature enough not to break in their hands.
(China was meadows flourishing with trees,
a willow province in the west, a province

35

wholly given to cypress in the south,
near the sea, in the eastern reaches, marshes
of salt scrub, fern, sea grass, the bamboo province,
in the north pine, a province dense with pine.)

The sticks were tapered, long, immensely graceful.
Down the length of each they would carve the forms
of buffalo, anemone, flamingo,
constellations ascending over China,
flowers and vines exploding into blossom,
a paradise of undergrowth, roots, wild life.

These whittled spears, these decorated slivers
of cypress, bamboo, willow, they would eat with,
allotting them that space between the fingers
for which no use had been devised before,
plunging the tips into small porcelain bowls
and, by a subtle flexing of the joints,
coming up with raw shrimp, fine noodles, bean curd.

III

The sage Wang Chung, in the first century,
records the story of the Viscount Chi-tse
weeping when the news reached him at the court
the Emperor Chou had used chopsticks of ivory.

He wept because jade cups were matched with ivory
and, by tradition, jade was to be used
only at functions where the menu listed
dragon liver and unborn leopard on it.
Now, while dragon liver made a fine meal,
even in those days it was hard to come by:
a cup of morsels would not be enough.

The Emperor would not be satisfied.
His mood would change, his facial muscles tighten;
he would begin that grinding of incisors,
his speech would falter, his complexion darken.

Think of the cry that echoed through the kingdom,
the trembling in the confines of the court,
pure ivory with pure jade, an old man's rage,
the sin of not enough and that of excess.
The Emperor could not be satisfied.

When word of ivory chopsticks reached the Viscount,
they were tears of foreboding Chi-tse wept.

I V
The sea, in China, was of great importance,
even in provinces bereft of coasts,
provinces which, twenty-seven days inland
from the great ports by horse, by caravan,
would struggle with the meaning of the sea;
in which, at twilight, children of the village,
put to bed as the stars rose, were instructed
patiently, by their fathers, night to night:

imagine blue, pure blue, breathe salt, say ocean,
dream the thing you have never dreamed, the sea.

Thinking of the salt strangeness of blue waters,
they pictured abstract concepts, like the future,
limitless, deep, incomprehensible,
washing over them wave on endless wave,
something as large as China, even larger,
distance that daylight would not see the end of,
nor twenty-seven daylights of the journey,
nor the next darkness, nor the darkness after.

What the sea came to mean was spelled tomorrow,
the possible on which one might set forth.

V
Desert, in China, was of vast importance.
Father, what is the desert? Desert, child,
is the length of the daylight we have traveled,

---

is the measure of darkness still to come.

From an early age they were taught in China
desert is what remains when one is stripped
of nonessentials, that which burns away
at high heat and at great cost to ourselves,
all that we did not want or wanted too much
(the sins, my child, of not enough, of excess),
that place of dust within us which assures us
here there is nothing further to desire.

V I
What did they have to do but count the stars?

Only in the more cultivated sectors
were there machines, hand tools, sophistications
of agriculture, trade, technology,
with which a man might occupy his life,
the first vague scratchmarks of small social units
taking warmth from each other, giving warmth.

Only in provinces possessing names
was there painting on silk, carving of statues,
the weaving of their dreams into whole cloth,
that need to say, and then to say again,
how it was here, what it was to be human.

But deep in the remotest provinces,
still too unknown and strange to have been named,
the sun was warmth, at night the fire was warmth
(that fierce magic just recently discovered).
In the plains they would sit and count the stars.
In the forest they sat and counted stars.
In the mountains, twenty-seven days far
from the great waves of surf, of history,
breaking on coasts too alien to envision,
they sat, they waited, they would count the stars.
No one knows what they dreamed there, if they dreamed.

VII

Father, what are the mountains? Mountains, child,
are what one waits in, where one learns to count,
that province in which walls were once begun
but, as with all things men start, never finished
(o, the blunderings into misadventure:
why could they not have sat and counted stars,
been patient, rock-fast, learned somehow to wait?),
twenty-seven days from a dream of waters,
twenty-seven nights from the nearest star.

At the Hotel Where the Long Dark Begins

It is five-fifteen in the afternoon.
Though I have never worn a watch, my watch
reads five on one hand, fifteen on the other.
It is autumn. The dark will soon be falling.

Others are waiting for me in the lobby.
In a limited sense what I want most
is to shower before going to dinner.
In the corridors they speak of Brazil.

From the window I see the little park
where the half-seen, the strange, originate.
One knows the dark will soon engulf the trees.
Strangers are waiting for me in the lobby.

Somehow one knows Brazil is far, quite far,
but the miles of the dark, when the dark falls,
miles it takes half the dream to cross, lie farther.
It will take all my strength, it seems, to tell you.

I do not ask you to come with me, I
say nothing of Brazil, I cannot know
who may be waiting for me in the lobby,
where the lobby is, if there is a lobby.

All my life I have entered with restraint
into those lives I loved more than my own.
How could I enter here other than softly?
Why should I travel now any less strangely?

What I know are these hands escaped from wrists
meant, as the dark increases, to contain them.
In the profoundest sense what I want most
is to know what one does here with one's life.

I will give up my shower, cancel dinner,
muffle incessant music of Brazil,
skirt the malingerers who lurk downstairs
awaiting, rumor has it, my arrival,

abandon each small, wayward expectation
of the merest description of their faces,
some first vague intimation of their hands,
turn back suggestions of their purpose with me.

It is five-fifteen in the afternoon.
The dusk comes deft and soon to this dim plain.
From the window I see the trees go down
one by one with the darkness that assails them.

On all sides, all sides now, evening begins.
Brazil sweeps the long corridors, Brazil.
No longer do these wrists hope to contain.
It will take all my strength, I sense, to tell you

I do not ask you to come with me, I
withhold all hint of music, I want most
not the names of the crew packing the lobby
but to know what to do here with my life.

How to Improve Your Personality

When, in June, you are driven to those suburbs
where the dark is just beginning to fall,
the air burdened with roses, where the wind
suggests only the echoings of absence,
where, through the years, trees have arranged themselves
at the sides of the road in avenues

where whisper after whisper takes you deeper
into the landscape of your destination;
when they usher you into the great house,
the car left in the driveway, the lawn crossed,
after the wait, the brief wait, in the dark,
someone coming some distance to the door;

when you follow into the paneled study,
find them picking at watermelon slices
at a round table, curtains not yet drawn,
lamps not yet lit, darkness now deeply falling;
after the introductions have been made,
after each of three daughters, wearing swimsuits,

blonde hair, white teeth, fierce suntans, practicing
into the darkness how to be cheerleaders,
into suburban darkness and beyond,
how to improve their personalities,
enters, where the dusk takes the turn to evening,
enters, one more beautiful than another;

when their father has asked them if they feel
cold in their costumes, darkness falling, falling,
and their grandfather promised a new car
to the eldest, next year, at graduation,
and when their aunt proposes tours of Europe
as her gift to them on their eighteenth birthdays,

you seat yourself, when asked to, at their table,
permit yourself, at last, to be seduced,
even perhaps assist in the seduction,
exchange flirtatious glances with the one
who looks at you with every word she speaks,
each blonde, white-toothed, fierce suntanned word she speaks.

Their father draws a curtain, lights a lamp.
Their mother passes watermelon slices.
And you, you feel the darkness closing in.
When, in June, you are driven to those suburbs
where the girls practice how to be cheerleaders
into early June darkness and beyond,

over and over let the cool night air
ride their long legs, sweep their backs, take their arms,
rehearse, time after time, the perfect stance,
gestures one senses sum an education,
the grammar of the wrist, the ankle's syntax,
over and over beat, inflection, tone;

when the talk at the table turns to cars,
to tours of Europe, to accommodations,
darkness all the while falling, closing in,
there is nothing, it seems, you find to say,
nothing you can offer of cars, of tours,
least of all, perhaps, of accommodations,

prepared to wait the dark out, and beyond,
without a curtain drawn, without a lamp lit,
needing to work on what must be improved,

---

ready to hear your wrists and ankles sing,
ready to have your life break into flame,
ready, even, to speak, if somewhere pressed to,

speak of the tours conducted through the mind
of those who wait, of those who cannot wait
because they do not know what they should wait for,
of those who will not see Peru again,
though one need not yet quite define Peru,
say what it may be to be late, too late,

come, at last, to the strangeness closing in,
whether it be darkness or education,
embark on longing as though it were music,
implying what can only be implied,
the matter of the air burdened with roses,
the grammar of the wrist, the ankle's syntax.

They look to you, you know, for more than this,
this silence in the dimness of June suburbs,
this weight of darkness slowly closing in.
Better, perhaps, to join them in the sweet grass
where the lawn slopes off gently past the house
into the dark of evenings still unfathomed,

evenings for which, as yet, no name exists,
the smell of roses burdening the air,
the avenues to what is possible
lined on both sides with trees sending up rumors,
with the wind right, enough to deafen you,
whisper by whisper, wave by leaf-drenched wave;

over and over practice the right stance,
if not the perfect, rage with wrists and ankles
until, imagine, bone begins to sing,
one by one learn the cars, pronounce the tours,
time after time rehearse accommodations,
the long, slow, arduous coming to terms;

night to night work on personality,
know what to say at evening, in the suburbs,
something all the while falling, closing in,
the watermelon slices deftly served,
a curtain drawn, a lamp lit, you in darkness
seduced by darkness, saying nothing, nothing.

Havana

The young Cuban at the parking garage,
taking in at a glance, one knowing glance,
questions of authenticity, of style,
the texture of my days, my life's credentials,

says he wishes he had the car I have,
claims it would all be possible with that,
all of it, only not in green, of course,
but in his lucky shade: canary yellow.

I would like to have seen, I say, Havana,
to have stood on the Malecón and watched
the darkness coming down, the first stars rising,
a full tide breaking, wave on Cuban wave.

You know the place? You know the Caribbean?
Those slow, tropical eyes, their northern habit
of indifference cast off, brighten, flutter,
study me, not the car, flesh out my life.

I answer more but less than yes or no:
Only here do I know it, only here,
pointing, with that, a finger to my head.
His eyes, once more, are rifling my credentials.

He has black hair, black eyes, pale olive skin,
wears a mustache matinee-idol style,
thin and well-groomed, to the tips of his mouth.
He smells vaguely of cars and perspiration.

I think of the young seals off Veradero
sporting among the sandy coves and inlets,
at home within their bodies, sleek and wet,
their black hair rainbow-colored in the sun.

To his assistant, who twice calls his name,
twice says he cannot find the pale blue Jaguar,
each time failing to capture his attention,
he turns, with irritation lectures him

in Spanish, in that liquid Cuban Spanish:
Can't you see this guy has a love for Cuba?
Can't you understand two men being civil?
Have the grace, at least, not to interrupt.

I am the one, throughout the conversation,
who, more than once, chooses to say the name
of the bleached city, or the dream, he comes from.
I have not yet heard it in Cuban Spanish.

When he retrieves the car, the one with which
all of it would be possible for him,
all of it, authenticity, true style,
more sumptuous even than Cuban Spanish,

should it come in the yellow of canaries,
at last, at last I bring myself to ask him
if, once, before I leave, he might pronounce it,
as though it were what each of us had come from

but, for reasons unknown to us, had lost,
like the assistant's pale, elusive Jaguar,
that place from which each of us had been exiled,
pronounce it for me once, just once: Havana.

Launched

This is the day, it seems, we leave for Europe.
Mother, beside me, wears perfume and furs.
Father, manning the front seat with my brother,
drives at a speed both dangerous and thrilling.

It is as though all the light in the world
breaks here on the expressway, fills the car.
The little fox dozing at Mother's neck
clamps its tail in its teeth to forge a circle.

My brother watches Father in command,
fastens his eyes on Father's ease and deftness,
his way with gears, his splendor in the turns.
I know my brother lusts to take the wheel.

Radioing ahead for proper clearance,
Father requests instructions from the pier.
The ship, of course, will not embark without us.
We will be there, he states, when we are there.

Father tells them My wife sits in the rear now,
swamped in furs to her throat against the cold.
My older son, beside me, dreams of driving.
My younger son sits dreaming of the sea.

My brother, thirteen, comes back to one question:
When will it be his time, his turn, to steer?
At the right place and moment it will happen,
but only at that moment, Father tells him.

But for us, the expressway is deserted.
All the light in the world now floods the car.
Father accelerates to third from neutral.
The speed we reach tastes perilous and sweet.

Gulls climb the sheer, blue cliffs of morning weather.
The port lies south of here, flanking the sea.
Europe is opera, sculpture, walks, pure theatre,
what avails, what is unavailing here.

Mother and I now clock the miles to voyage.
Father heads south, resplendent to the teeth.
My brother, thirteen, hungry, dreams his one dream:
to sleep with all machines, to man all wheels.

My concern is with those we leave behind now.
What will they do without us, in our absence?
Mother, perfumed and furred, will reassure me:
Father, of course, has business to attend to;

my brother, she goes on, will be at school,
preparing, as she puts it, for his future.
I alone know his lust, know what he lusts for,
alone suspect that nothing can prepare us.

My brother circles back to time, to timing:
when, what year, will it be that he can drive?
My brother, thirteen, brown-eyed, is impatient.
Mother sings Preparation, Father Wait.

When I speak, dimension preoccupies me.
How far is France, I ask, how wide is England?
Where does the world end? Do we dream at sea?
Europe is where you find it, Father states.

My brother, brown-eyed, thinks he spies the liner.
I seek it slow and deep, not fast and free.

_____

The dazzle of the inner harbor blinds me.
Flame, the intensest flame, now rings the car.

Father, normally cautious, guns the motor.
Speed, of course, is what matters, speed, pure speed.
All of it, light, air, water, shapes a circle,
the one the fox grips fiercely in his teeth.

Scriabin

It will be told, of course, in the detail.
The wind will whistle through the cracks, the nails
chafe at the bondage of confirmed positions,
the cup quite nearly sing in a plain saucer
before the fire on Russian afternoons,

pleased to have warmth suffusing its thin glaze.
Even the house, predictable, familiar,
leaning this way or that, burdened with years,
longs to throw off the torpor of old habits,
cast its lot with upheaval, revolution.

Under weather which falls on all the Russias,
one has only to sit here, listen, wait,
study one's hands as though they too were set
slowly adrift from memory, from feeling,
deprived of the small heat of one's existence.

Whiteness is our undoing: to be Russian
must mean one shall have learned in time to suffer
white at the heart of everything that matters:
fieldscape, horizon, silence, afternoon,
private music, the dreams of snowy evenings.

Except that one forgets just why one waits,
forgets even the need to have remembered,
forgets the place, how one reaches this place
from wherever it is one starts, forgets
its name, the white wine of its name, forgets

what it is to remember making progress
logically, dimly, step by Russian step,
into that life of voyages, of choices,
where it is given us to know men choose.
One lives the life they live in all the Russias,

letting the weather come down, as it must,
letting the evening find us, if it finds us,
blinded in fields, cold hamlets, at the heart
of some forgotten strangeness where our breathing
almost requires of us no more than breathing,

paying little attention to the cracks,
music pouring from cracks, pure blaze in cups,
the vigil of the nails, detail, detail,
anarchy plotting richly in the floorboards,
conspiracies of rot toppling old forms.

What does one do with one's life in the evening?
Dusk on the road that slashes through the country
of our regret, of our forgetfulness,
falls not like dusk but like a desolation,
that aching slant, that groaning of the nets,

that sifting, grain by grain, of loathsome salts
(indoors, one plans fierce study of the hands),
the smoke of Russian grates staining the air,
suspended in provincial skies like questions
forever on the verge of being asked.

At the Château de Villegenis That Summer

"Mrs. W. E. Corey playing cards with the wounded officers on the porch, Château de Villegenis at Palaiseau, France, September 18, 1918. Mrs. Corey, or Mabelle Gilman, an actress, was the wife of the president of Carnegie Steel Company and United States Steel."

In long white gloves and matching white silk frock,
the tunic gathered, pleated, the skirt shirred,
Mrs. Corey plays whist this afternoon
at Palaiseau, glittering in the half-light
cast by the little sun-porch where she sits,

officers in dress uniform her guests,
the sun streaming beyond them, through the leaves,
one wing of the mansion visible, gleaming
softly through willows, eight cards in her hand
splayed as deftly as though she held a fan.

On the porch are arranged tub after tub
of ivy, sedum, phlox, nightshade, laburnum,
scene after woodland scene depicted on them,
trellis by trellis tableaux to the floor.
Beyond, the light falls slowly from the trees.

Mrs. Corey has opened the château
this season to those needing quiet, rest,
those whom, by now, she may well call "our wounded."
The hospital committee has a list
from which the names, all summer, have been drawn.

Across the little wicker table from her,
seated in wicker chairs which match precisely,
are youths she whiles the afternoon away with,
men unremarkable but for the calm
each seems to have brought with him, the spent light.

Perhaps at the photographer's suggestion,
two pretend to be studying their cards
("correspondence to life" he may have called it)
with a concentration so fixed, so pure,
a scrutiny so close, so undivided,

deuces and Jacks seem less than worthy of it.
The third man folds his cards against his lap,
surveys the choices laid out here before him,
ponders matters of strategy and risk,
tries to remember what has been discarded.

Mrs. Corey gazes into the camera,
her body shifting subtly in her chair
so that, at the degree she has achieved,
she can be seen as both player of whist
with wounded officers and, at the same time,

a beauty wholly conscious of a camera
prowling the outer limits of the sun-porch,
coming at last to take up its position
perhaps not more than five or six feet from her.
How delicately light falls from the trees.

Perhaps it is the drama of her hat
in contrast to the bare heads of the soldiers,
heads made by half-light even more austere,
which proves, for all this radiance, unsettling:
Italian lattice-work trimmed with organza,

its lines voluptuous, its angles soaring,
brim wide enough to shield her from the sun
should a cue come to move into the sun,
silk sash gracing a chin as eloquent
as any play she may have spoken lines in.

Whether, each afternoon, she lets them win,
whether the cards she plays, or fails to play,

can be considered kindness, deferential
in the extreme, cannot now be determined.
It is not that they lack technique or skill,

but the eyes close, or can close, in an instant,
in the heat of the bidding a tongue stammers,
a head nods, or a hand begins to quiver,
an arm, quite inexplicably, goes numb,
a breeze stirs in the willow, a leg twitches,

fever flushes a cheek, the body trembles,
perspiration assails a lip, a palm,
or the gaze wanders off to a bird scrawling
passionate, living signs across a sky
too blinding, too immense, to be searched further.

Placed to her right, his head recently shaved,
a man wears a dressing taped to his skull,
concealing where the scalpel plunged, the sutures.
One knows the place and nature of the wound,
or thinks one knows. Looking at the torn head,

one knows, or claims to know, the thing he suffers.
One knows nothing, nothing, of what he suffers.
One pinpoints pain, one guesses at impairment.
One specifies the damage, then moves on.
How intricately light falls from the trees.

But it is the others the eye seems drawn to,
the ones whose heads still sport full growths of hair,
those who wear no bandages, show no scars,
those in whom one looks elsewhere for their wounds,
eyes averted, refusing to engage

whatever it may be the eyes engage,
even casually, those Mrs. Corey
invites this afternoon for conversation,

strolls in the garden, views of summer, whist,
later, shadows filtering through the grass,

a girl, apron and starched white maid's cap dazzling,
crossing the lawn before them, summer fading,
bearing a tray of jam cakes and green tea,
wisps of red hair escaping from her cap
catching what light falls late from the great trees.

One soldier rests a small hand on his thigh.
A watch strapped to the wrist looms from a shirtcuff
not quite long enough to insure concealment.
Here, at once, from the moment you first see it,
here, from this pale-eyed man's ill-fitting shirt,

its sleeve not covering all a sleeve covers,
here, with this steel chronometer whose hands
seem suddenly too heavy, too explicit,
the numbers staring from the face too bold,
the sun striking the crystal cold, too cold,

tea served, or not served, cakes passed, never passed,
beyond, late summer fragrant in the trees,
you have the thing you need, or think you need;
you know all injury must lie with that;
you touch the wound, intact: time passed, time passing.

When they go back, what is it they go back to?:
the Soldiers' Home; the convalescent sections,
corridors reeking with the smells of loss
and disinfectant, equally ferocious;
wards where the air is stained with cries they smother,

unsuccessfully, in their sweat-soaked pillows,
dreaming, though sleepless, of the life before this,
who one was, what one longed for, bits made whole,
tracing the vague outline of obscure faces,
repeating, but in whispers, some lost name,

remembering, but dimly, dimly now,
the lawn, the light, the visionary trees,
the hat the hostess wore at some château
far from here, the maid's burning hair still bringing
to their lips one word, just one: conflagration.

Evening, at Palaiseau, need not be mentioned.
The subject of the dark need not be broached.
Mrs. Corey arranges that the bus
return guests to the hospital by dusk
(the night falls long and steep on this estate),

believing it is better for them elsewhere,
cared for by others, doctors, staff, attendants,
amused, comforted, fed, served tea, distracted,
the first stars rising once they have departed,
the moon, the willow, bright beyond their wards,

the portents, though pervasive, less apparent
than they would be, and are, at the château,
where, with the weight of darkness as momentous,
as perilous, as anything they dream,
the lawn fills quickly, quickly, the sea spreads.

Better, too, they be spared those agitations:
the cards played, or the cards not played, from kindness,
what one took to be kindness (consolation
and sunlight, someone said, can bring them back);
the scowl that roils the brow of the old King;

the beauty of the mask worn by the Queen;
one last, however grandiose attempt
to keep from them that final desolation:
how treacherous the grass here has become,
how deep the strait from porch to house and back.

My Father Deep and Late on the Route South

My father, driving south, cries out "Romance,"
not at all certain that we understand.
In the rear, too dim to identify,
too indistinct to see, or be seen, clearly,
are the others, myself, it seems, among them.

My father, on the route south, cries "Romance,
it was romance I wanted," his eyes turning
from the road, which has opened out before us,
to the ones in the rear, who travel with him.
Tears are now spilling slowly to his cheeks.

It is a day in winter. Light comes down
as it is bound to come down this far south,
this late in a lost winter, on my father:
sumptuously, at least until the dusk falls.
Light fills his hands, his words go up in smoke.

Though it has been some time since we first set out,
it seems I may not know where we are going,
though that is not important. Just to be here,
here with my father driving, the ice blinding,
in pursuit of the route called the route south,

aware, however dimly, of the power
of distance, daybreak, mileage, destinations,
the magic lodged in simply setting out
in a dawn of late winter, words turned smoke,
may be all I want, all I ever wanted.

The others ride oblivious, unfazed,
seem, for some reason, to ignore his tears,
to see nothing of what subverts his face,
though their preference may be not to notice,
to peer for landmarks, say, or gape at landscape.

Of those traveling south here with my father,
crammed in the rear, ambiguous, unfocused,
the crew, though unidentified, he turns to
when, at last, it is time for him to turn,
it is I, placed so that nothing escapes me,

only I, in these loss-struck miles, who hears him,
I, only I, who sees his tears are tears,
myself alone, feaster on light, forever
sniffing out embarkations down the wind,
haunted, incessantly, by words ("horizons"),

cold now, and small, invisible, or nearly,
and yet acutely, too acutely, present,
child in whose cold, small hands the light is jammed,
who knows precisely what my father suffers
(though I do not yet know how I can know it),

crying one word, one word, on the route south,
I alone who studies that dream-wracked face
as though it were the tale of my own life
unfolding: tears in winter, words becoming
smoke, the moment one has managed to speak them,

smoke, should one turn when it is time to turn,
regaling those one comes with, bleak, bedraggled
(none of whom, in the rear, one knows, or can know,
none of whom can be seen, beside me, clearly),
with those cries of "Romance" on the route south,

strangers, admittedly, the whole dim crew,
yet the very ones one's fate is to cross with,

ice glittering from here to the first stars,
the ones who come this far since it is cold
and there seems nowhere else for them to come,

drawn by my father's fervor at the wheel,
the drama of departure and goodbye,
lured by the warmth, implied warmth, of the route,
any route, leading south, stunned by the cry
my father, in the quiet, turns to cry.

(Do all fathers, in time, cry out "Romance,"
turning to small, cold sons artfully propped
in small, cold seats behind them to miss nothing,
turning as though the turn might be sufficient
to explain tears, to articulate anguish?

Do all fathers, their hands spilling with light,
hold to the wheel so richly, take command,
set out at dawn, the route (by implication)
to who one is, to what is possible,
fixed in their heads, o voyagers, like music?)

It is a day in winter. In the car,
cramped as we are, confined, waving farewell,
the weather, like my father, constant, clear,
everything one might need to start one's life,
to start it here, presents itself, and amply:

a father doubling, deftly, as the driver,
a genius of direction, dedication,
tooling south with a true feel for the wheel
but an even truer feel for the way,
and a horizon (any will do) to which

we drive all day, since someone knows the way,
or seems to know the way, which is the same,
anticipation building in proportion

---

not to the claims made (he has none to make)
but to what he declines, all day, to say.

It seems my father knows what no one else knows:
why, of all roads to hold to, of all freeways
to be inching along one dazzling morning,
assailed by light, by ice, by expectation,
it is this route we follow, the route south;

why, of the words which one might cry, or has cried,
of the words one may yet be moved to cry,
deep in the miles of some late, frozen crossing,
one alone of the many, one, just one,
holds the power to bring tears to his eyes;

why, of all things to want, to be found wanting,
of all one might at last divulge to strangers,
those with whom, for some reason, one has come,
nondescript in the rear, but here, aware
largely of landscape, if aware of that,

of all, beneath this sky, one turns to say
when it is time to turn, to say, he says
one word, "Romance," pronouncing it as though,
dim in the rear, cold, small, immensely blinded,
someone has almost asked our destination.

At the Border

"President Fernando Belaunde Terry of Peru with
soldiers at a remote jungle post recaptured from Ecuador"

At the border this is what it will be,
this, if you close your eyes, the very texture
of "jungle," yes, but "remote" jungle, too,
fly-speck on a map of the deep, the sultry,

both the scene made plain and the scene imagined,
everywhere tree-vines looping overhead,
everywhere light, near light, far light, light falling,
details of growth, of undergrowth, heat-glare,

green floor of untracked forest overgrown
beyond one's power to tell what is floor
and what, the greater part, anarchy rampant,
mountains to one side, river to the other,

a breeze, at dusk, moving south from the Andes,
the nearest settlement hundreds of miles
upwind, or down (clearly not near at all),
should distance here submit to calculation,

an interior no one cared to notice,
no one suspected mattered, one lost hectare
more, or one less, of looping vines, until,
one morning, dawn bleaching the capital,

old men raking street-dust with wisps of brooms,
the clamor swept those corridors, that structure
with Justice, classically proportioned, chiseled
on a marble pediment cut to last

at least a generation, but now crumbling,
within, the fan-blades droning overhead,
the whisper of official papers, shuffled,
shuffled again, echoing through the halls.

Spanish lies so heavily on the air,
that and the smoke of carbines, you can smell it,
hold it against the light everywhere pouring
to trace, through haze, the markings of the verbs.

The platoon sergeant-major is escorting
the President along the front, forgetting
there is nothing as solid as a front
between his men and theirs, all is in flux,

forgetting, too, or not having remembered,
where Peru begins and Ecuador ends
has always been, will always be, in doubt,
the precise here or there to be determined

to the satisfaction of no one famished
for the consolations of fixed positions,
borders, marked and unmarked, definite stances.
Only the trees are certain, if the trees.

The President will smile, will bid the troops
Good Day, or Fine Job, Men, or something like that,
but much richer in Peruvian Spanish
than whatever I might attribute to him,

weighted with the grammar of history,
cadences struck in latitudes where light
slams too long and too hard, rages at angles
a less resistant tongue would wither under.

Battle-gear held aloft, muscles relaxed,
a thatched hut in the background their command post,

the troops, for their part, know only to smile,
responsive to the smile that they are met with,

as they await new orders, fresh deployments,
know, for some reason, to stand in the sun
coming down as it comes down nowhere else
this morning, eyes bright, faces flushed, triumphant,

pretending, or convinced, it has to do
with the glory of what some call Peru,
some Ecuador, depending on the light,
on how the wind moves south across the Andes,

pretending, or convinced, it lies with winning,
that, but for one more tract, green heaped on green,
unfathomed, and unfathomable, floor,
we can hold long to things, things can be won.

The President, still smiling, caught between
abstract concepts like honor, valor, justice,
and the specific need, throughout the tour,
to appear nothing less than presidential,

asks each man where he comes from, grasps each hand,
speaks of what, without question, will be owed them
once the disputed sectors are secured.
The light comes down, the vines persist in growing.

The troops, for their part, stand beneath the sun,
at least until some new command is given,
until the President returns to Lima,
pronounce, merely by standing there, the theme,

the grand theme, of the Spanish-speaking poets
at posts as overgrown, as drenched, as this
(waiting is the name of the thing we suffer),
not knowing just by standing they pronounce it,

perspiring in their uniforms, the six-day
beards on their faces lengthening to seven,
the heat pressing relentlessly on shoulders
you see are the shoulders of boys, not men,

their smiles held (and still holding), on the air,
tremulous air, their Spanish looped like vines,
ponderous, green, the nouns drawn out, extended,
the thing one looks for, struggles with, divisions,

nowhere ascertainable between one part
of the configuration and another,
nowhere differentiations of jungle
and jungle outpost, outpost and command post,

eyes closed, or half-closed (or perhaps not either),
Ecuador hazy, taken for Peru,
Peru, the true Peru, in question, too
(the trees alone know, if even the trees),

smiles held, or smiles still holding, definitions
unclear, at best, or guessed, momentous chaos
of brush, of underbrush, of light, of half-light,
floor-meeting-sky, sky-meeting-floor, the door

to honor, valor, justice, love of country,
opening, on the farther side, to need,
the President taking each hand, still smiling,
the breeze we thought might move south from the Andes,

cooling us, the mere shuffling and reshuffling
of official papers far off in Lima,
or the scrape of the broom against the street,
light eating marble, marble eating light,

the platoon's shoulders glinting in the sun
(or could it be their gear?), the theme, the grand theme,

stamped for all time across each soldier's languor,
nowhere to be seen apart from the rest,

the other themes, or grand themes, those distinctions
of made plain and imagined, demarcations
between the border and the Spanish for it,
nowhere visible in this weather, nowhere.

Waiting for Marguerite

The train will never come, as one well knows,
which will be why the painting must be called
Waiting for Marguerite, or simply Waiting.

From the outset, from the look of a sky
much too clear, much too flawless, for a sky,
from the shimmering weightlessness of objects

in which all things seem able to drift off,
without a moment's warning, into vapor,
into the endless echoings of absence,

one knows it to be wrong, or out of place,
or, all the while one travels through it, dreaming.
Waiting for Marguerite it must be called.

A double track stretches from here to there
(returns not yet wholly unthinkable
the implication is, though all else may be)

into an outcome not yet quite foreclosed,
vanishing seamlessly on a horizon
as airless, thin, and blue as it is here,

where each stop down the line, if there are stops,
the repetition deafening, relentless,
bears the same name, the same name: Disappear.

There is no sun, no moon, there are no stars,
but the station's facade, boards, windows, walls,
leaks with a spare, pure light, its source unknown.

Even, off to one side, the baggage dolly,
drawn to the platform when a train is due,
wears the silence of its abandonment

beautifully, silhouetted against a sky
asking nothing of us and giving nothing,
its proportions, at dusk, quite perfect, just,

though, properly, its two wheels should be four
in the name of all things which may be real,
the spokes not be forever free of dust.

Her name is Marguerite. She will not come,
nor would she come with luggage, if she came,
bags a porter would hoist onto the dolly

if, in fact, the station boasted a porter
(all stops here bear the same name: Disappear),
if the dolly had not two wheels but four.

A tailless, white toy bulldog, green eyes fixed
in the direction from which the express
would come, if the express came, holds its ground,

peers, like the man beside him, down the track,
its paws set delicately at the rail's edge,
waits with a patience dog-like yet undog-like,

straining, as a dog will, to sniff arrivals,
the lost, fierce smell of them, on a blue wind,
trembling at the sound of remembered thunder.

His master, with the same transparent eyes,
waits, too, for what one knows will never come,

stands with a grace, an ease, the left knee bent,

hands clasped behind his back holding a dozen
long-stemmed wild beauties meant for Marguerite
the moment she debarks from the express,

true daisies of the field which, in the chaos
of their impassioned preparation, seem
too orderly for flowers, trail no scent.

Slender, tall, with black trousers and black jacket
over fresh, starched white shirtfront and black bow-tie,
he wears a brush mustache, a captain's hat,

wears the look of a man who, every evening,
when the first stars would rise, if there were stars,
sets out from his grey house, across dry fields,

into a dusk that gathers on all sides
(gathers and, though unwitnessed by us, deepens),
who, each time, by odd routes and combinations

of circuitous short-cuts through the outskirts,
finds himself here, in the vicinity
of the tracks, a man who, could it be known,

comes with a fresh bouquet to meet a train
certain to arrive by the time the dark falls,
a train even his dog catches a whiff of,

the last train on this run, the late express,
speeding from Disappear to Disappear,
one which may or may not have stopped here once,

once, for some reason stricken from the schedule,
the train which Marguerite may well have boarded
in the smoke of a distant, dream-wracked city.

His ambition may be simply to move her,
simply to be moved by her (which he is),
simply to stand and wait in expectation

of what may yet be possible, of what
darkness and separation may yet work,
those incongruities of tone and texture

one calls, or would call, life (though one well knows
the darkness in this painting waits to fall,
never falls, knows the train will never come),

simply to see those legs flash from her skirt
as she steps to the platform from the coach,
pressing wild daisies to her chest, perceiving

their fragrance as the sweetest in the world,
needing neither to cry out Porter, Porter,
nor, unanswered, seek assistance with luggage,

here so that, at last, he might move her, move her,
so that he might give what he has to give,
daisies, or self, or darkness, here because

this, rider, is as far as one can go,
this is where the signs read Annulled, Annulled.
Her name is Marguerite. She will not come.

River Road

Running off with the boy at the gas station,
yellow-haired, clear-eyed, with a pair of hands
nothing, you understand, would prove too much for,
is, it seems, a simple enough solution.

Consequences never enter your thinking
at the start. Whatever the implications
of the act, of the speed with which you act,
all one knows, and all one chooses to know,

is summed in this: we are to be together.
On River Road, the great elms overhead
branch out to shape a tunnel which we race through
as we make our escape, leaf-dappled, late,

the avenue to what is possible,
water on one side, deep woods on the other.
The water's depth goes down in feet and inches,
but the depth of the woods is only guessed.

Driving all night, deeper into the country,
we pause at dawn, finding a roadside shack
which serves us what we call a wedding breakfast,
homemade raspberry tarts and lemon ices.

I remember that first glimpse of him, sprawled
over the body of a green coupé,
feverish, rapt, all ardor, lean, committed,
almost making love, it seemed, to the engine.

The yellow hair hung down across his eyes,
damp and limp with the sweat beading his forehead.
Two arms lodged elbow-deep within the gearshaft,
the hands, when you saw hands, the awesome gifts

not of a boy who haunted the gas station
but of a man for whom one understands
nothing, in time, will be impossible,
motor, transmission, fan-belt, valves, a life.

Illumination from a single light bulb
beat down across the muscles of his back.
Beyond him, from the body shop, there leaked
darkness to match those woods whose depth one guesses.

Every night since then, since River Road
and the tunnel through which, quite late, we fled,
I find him sprawled over another chassis
left to his care in a garage with one bulb

by someone who knows what those hands can do,
knows, or has heard, what can be worked with love,
suspects (I am not able to say how)
nothing will not be possible for him,

passionate with attention, with concern,
held by the task at hand as he is held
by nothing in this life here, here, together,
yellow hair in his eyes, light on his back.

Knowing no longer what it is I want,
flayed by the memory of what I wanted,
the possible, the uses of the hands,
the uses, later, deeper, of the body,

I think of River Road turning to moonlight
beneath the lyric hissing of the tires,

moonlight becoming water, water woods,
everything turning much too deep to guess,

fragrance on all sides pinning us beneath it.
sweet avenue to the nights stretched before us.
It may come down to this: one's choice of route.
It may be that, at dusk, when the moon rises,

when, for the thousandth time, the dark begins
what it seems to know no end of beginning,
the stars strung in the branches, River Road
cut at an angle somehow penetrating

the countryside of all we dream and long for,
the heart of our location, of romance,
two others, quite unknown to us, their crankcase
worked to perfection, brakes fixed for endurance,

their tires aligned to yield both speed and distance,
bearings retooled to make good their escape,
engine fitted to lead them down that route
almost without their need to steer, to choose,

set out this evening, late, on River Road,
that avenue to what is possible,
water on one side, deep woods on the other
lovelier for the depths they would withhold,

seeming to know precisely what the miles know,
seeming to choose to go where the road goes.
Knowing the risk involved now and the price
of wild raspberry tarts and lemon ices,

the sting, at dawn, of sour and sweet at once
exotic to the tongues of two so young,
two who have driven all night, running off,
the spill of moonlight drenching River Road,

---

the same fierce angle, the same penetration,
I need to think again how deep the woods run
(what lies beyond, of course, a myth, a guess),
I need to weigh the cost of staying home.

After the Reading

Dear Mr. Hecht: Having somehow assumed,
earlier in my life, that the beginnings
one makes, or does not quite make, bear the portents
of all that follows, intricate, detailed,
perhaps I can begin this letter to you
by speaking of the student's violin case
propped at an outer wall, just where we entered
this evening, late in March, nestled beside
a sheaf of scores, duos with flute, sonatas,
the name of the composer, F. J. Haydn,
etched in black on a ground so dense, so yellow,
light seemed to flood the stairs, leak to the lobby,
spill to the little folding metal chairs
arranged precisely for the poet's reading.
I felt the sun bear down, I thought of Rome,
light, at noon, drenching those deserted gardens.
I smelled the dust of 1951.
I thought, too, that the student had long hair,
hair reaching to her waist and chestnut color.
I thought she may have hurried from her lesson,
taking the gravel path, the path we took,
looking up at a sky now jammed with stars
(earlier it had rained), the branches leafless,
running the last few paces, library steps
taken two at a time, wanting to miss
nothing of what you might read, not a line,
wanting to be present from the beginning,
her movement from one music to another,
hair flying, the grass wet, a half-moon rising,
pleasing me, as I hope it pleases you.

After the violin case I would speak of
that photo of you, 1951.
You are in Rome that year, I in Virginia,
having come by Chesapeake and Ohio
from New York with my mother, then Bay ferry,
staying at the house of two spinster cousins
to spend three days in Norfolk with my brother,
stationed nearby at Little Creek that winter.
Though we came for the weekend, I remember
what seems day after day passed on the sun-porch
watching the noontime strollers crossing Granby,
working out, or attempting to work out,
on the Bechstein (my cousins taught piano)
intricacies of fingering, of phrasing,
in the Scarlatti brought to Norfolk with me,
leafing through magazines Tillie and Bess
stacked beside the avocado and date-palm.
It was in one of these I found your picture
in an article featuring Accomplished
Young Americans, your face one of several,
the caption mentioning the Prix de Rome,
the first, it claimed, awarded to a poet.

The Roman light, pressing across your shoulders,
moving in from the leaves that frame your face,
spills to the very border of the picture,
fills the folds of the shirt you wear, a white shirt,
so immensely, I smell the dust it raises.
I feel it break in waves against my back.
(I may not have known light looked quite like that,
could look like that, or else I had forgotten.)
The strollers pass on Granby, bent on missions
passionate, weighty, deathless, who can say?
My cousins teach piano, turn the date-palm
mornings and afternoons to face a sun
as mild, as tender, as the way they turn.
You wait in a garden, small-boned and dark.
I do not yet know what it is you wait for,

nor do I seem, that year, able to guess,
though I may think that, with sufficient patience,
or strength, or something I cannot yet name,
it will, in time, be given me to know.
Nor do I yet know what "a poet" is,
but your head is so dark against these leaves,
the leaves themselves so shapely, so resplendent,
Rome so fierce, so extravagant, a presence,
and your shirt, as I say, so wholly blinding,
these, for now, will seem poetry enough.
What a fever of sunlight, what a burning.

Having first asked permission of my cousins,
I take the scissors from the heart-shaped wicker
sewing basket perched on the little sun-porch
between the avocado and the date-palm,
I, who have brought Scarlatti south to Norfolk,
I, who struggle with fingering, with phrasing,
through the weekend, preoccupied with wrist work,
pedaling, shading, plotting strategies
of approach, of seduction, all that day,
seeking somehow to take by sheer surprise
whatever meaning glitters from those measures,
approaching from the rear, say, from the side,
making small progress through the difficulties
(and they are many) built into the score,
making my way, almost making my way,
from one long, dark, slow music to another,
from D. Scarlatti to A. Hecht, "a poet,"
as I cut from the magazine your picture
(and with it word of Rome, of light itself,
of "poetry," whatever that may be),
insert it carefully between two pages
of the sonata I will take back with me
on the Chesapeake and Ohio Sunday
evening, after my brother's leave expires,
after Tillie and Bess, my grey-haired cousins
who teach piano in a house on Granby,

77

for one last time that day, with the dusk falling,
turn the date-palm to face the morning sun.
Sleepless, I ride the night coach to New York,
dreaming of darkness, light, entrances, Rome.

Earlier, as I mentioned, it had rained here.
The gravel path we take, the same we came by,
gleams in the dark with remnants of small pools
which light our way through the deserted campus.
It is late March; the sky is jammed with stars,
spring stars, as I remember having told you,
and we go back, some to their dormitories,
some to their cars, students of violin,
students of 1951 alike,
back to the dream, or life, which occupied us
before we came to hear you read this evening,
committed to the fingering, the phrasing,
in pursuit of an entrance into meaning
(just one, just one, however tenuous,
unpromising, or meager at the start),
an opening to pure speech, to one's life,
to what may still be possible, to rhythms
as instinctive as breathing, perhaps more so,
an approach (from the rear, say, from the side)
subtle, slow, forceless, almost inadvertent,
so that we take loveliness by surprise
late one evening, if we take it at all.

The gabled house on Granby has new tenants,
a shipyard fitter, his wife, three young children;
what light the spindly date-palm turns to face
leaks from the television on the sun-porch,
droning on and on through those afternoons
of thick, grey skies and game shows whose first prize
will be a flight to Rome on Alitalia.
Tillie and Bess play Bach beneath Miami,
those four-hand duets, from sleek bronze coffins
as imposing as they themselves were frail

(the depth at which they lie muffles their tones),
though I would tell you, too, that, of their pupils,
one is half a conglomerate in Tulsa
(oil, I believe), one overdosed on Chopin
in a hotel room overlooking Venice,
one, for some reason, ran off to Brazil,
and, as I remember, none has the name
Vladimir Horowitz stamped in his passport.
The Bechstein sold at auction to a dealer
in antique instruments and what his card called
"curiosities of a life in music."
My brother came to nothing, dead of wounds
sustained not in that war but in this life.

You, too, go back: to Rochester, New York,
whose winters you described, two or three times,
as difficult, or worse. Is there a sun-porch
somewhere in Rochester, a date-palm on it
turned mornings, afternoons, to face the sun?
From those half-opened windows, do you hear
pupils practicing scales these mild, clear evenings,
the dark fragrant with hints of Schumann, Brahms?
Are there still spinsters giving piano lessons,
vigilant that the wrists be elevated
and the tone melting, that the foot bear lightly
treading the splendid mysteries of the pedal?
Do students of the violin there prop
violin cases against lobby walls,
and Haydn sing out from fierce yellow backgrounds?
Is the sky jammed with stars there, does the path
glitter with small, dark pools after the rain?
What of the light: can you say if the sun
hammers your shoulders now as it did then,
thirty years ago, in a Roman garden?
Does the light rage in Rochester, New York?
Is there fever to speak of, is there burning?
How does the dark come down there? Slowly? Deep?
Can you tell me what thirty years was like:

---

a week, a month, an instant, thirty years?
Do you remember 1951,
even, some nights, feel sheer affection for it?
Does the dust of it rise to meet you, mornings?
Is there a boy leafing through magazines there,
idling away the weekend on a sun-porch,
preoccupied with fingering, with phrasing,
strategies, campaigns, ways into the music
beyond the mere, spare signals the notes give,
taught light because it was light you would teach,
awake on the night coach barreling north
haunted by Rome, by "poetry," by leaves
so dark, so bright, so complex in their clusters,
he cannot yet be certain, all that night,
through the days after, where foliage ends
and, against it, Anthony Hecht begins?

PS3563 087434 P4 1983
+Peru / Herbert M+Morris, Herbert,

0 00 02 0209888 5
MIDDLEBURY COLLEGE